RED MEANS GO

Red Means Go

TONY MEDLEY

CONTENTS

First Printing, 2025

Printed in the United States of America

ISBN (Paperback): 979-8-9934305-7-7
ISBN (eBook): 979-8-9934305-8-4

Publisher:
Medley Publishing Group

Cover Design: Tony Medley
Interior Design & Layout: Tony Medley

Scripture References:
Unless otherwise noted, Scripture quotations are from the Holy Bible, New King James Version®, copyright © 1982 by Thomas Nelson. Used by permission. All rights reserved.

Disclaimer:
This book is intended for spiritual and personal development. It is not a substitute for professional counseling, therapy, medical care, or legal advice. Readers are encouraged to seek qualified professionals when needed.

Preface

There are moments in life when it feels like everything has come to a screeching halt. The weight of mistakes, regrets, and missed opportunities can sit on our shoulders like a red light that never turns green. Maybe you've been there—you wanted to move forward, but shame told you to stay stuck. You tried to believe in yourself, but the echoes of condemnation reminded you of your failures.

But I have good news: Jesus Christ specializes in turning red lights into green lights. His shed blood not only forgives your sin but also empowers you to rise again.

That's why this book is called Red Means Go. In the world's traffic system, red means stop. In Heaven's system of grace, red means go.

The blood of Jesus speaks a better word over your life. It says you are free, forgiven, redeemed, and destined for greatness. No matter where you have been, what you have done, or how many times you have fallen, God's mercy is stronger. He is not finished with you.

This book was written in a life-coaching style so that you can not only read about freedom but also practice it, apply it, and walk it out daily. At the end of each chapter, you will find reflection questions, declarations, and practical steps to help you live in victory. My prayer is that every page pushes you past hesitation and into acceleration.

You don't have to stay at the red light of shame any longer. Through the blood of Jesus, the light has changed. Red means go!

— Dr. Tony F. Medley Sr.

Introduction

The story that frames this book is found in John 8:1–11, when a woman was caught in adultery and dragged before Jesus by a crowd eager to stone her. According to the law, she deserved punishment. According to the crowd, she had no future. According to her own guilt, she was disqualified.

But then Jesus stepped into the scene. Instead of condemning her, He silenced her accusers. Instead of agreeing with the law's demand for death, He offered her the gift of life. His final words to her were simple yet life-changing:

"Neither do I condemn you; go and sin no more."

Notice what Jesus did not say. He did not say, "Sit here in shame." He did not say, "Live the rest of your life trying to pay for your mistake." He did not say, "Your destiny is over." He said, "Go."

The blood of Jesus gives us permission to move forward when life tells us to stop. It gives us courage to dream again after failure, strength to rebuild after loss, and hope to step into a future bigger than our past.

This book is not written to theologians or scholars, though they may benefit from it. It is written to people like you and me—people who have missed the mark, fallen short, and wondered if they could ever recover. It is written to believers who need a reminder that God's grace doesn't just clean the slate, it empowers the next step.

In these pages, you will discover how the blood of Jesus transforms "red light" moments into green light opportunities. You will learn to see your mistakes as setups for your miracle. You will receive tools to turn shame into momentum and failure into fuel for your destiny.

So buckle up, because Red Means Go is not just a message—it is a movement. A movement away from condemnation and into calling. A movement away from guilt and into grace. A movement away from paralysis and into purpose.

The light has changed. Are you ready to go?

Dedication

This book is dedicated to every person who has ever felt stuck at the red light of shame, regret, or failure.

To those who believed their mistakes disqualified them, their past defined them, or their future was canceled—this is for you.

May these pages remind you that through the blood of Jesus, the red that once meant stop now means go.

I also dedicate this work to my family, whose love and support continue to fuel my journey, and to the countless men and women of faith who have modeled resilience, grace, and courage. Your lives are proof that God's green light is always brighter than life's red lights.

Acknowledgements

I would like to express my deepest gratitude to God, whose mercy, grace, and power inspired every word of this book. Without His voice, there would be no message.

To my family—thank you for believing in me and standing with me in every season of life and ministry. Your prayers and encouragement are treasures I carry in my heart.

To my friends, mentors, and ministry partners—you have sharpened, challenged, and strengthened me along the way. Your influence has shaped this work more than you know.

To my readers—thank you for opening your hearts to this journey. You are the reason I write, teach, and coach. My prayer is that Red Means Go will ignite courage in you, renew your hope, and move you boldly into your God-given destiny.

And finally, to Jesus Christ—my Redeemer, my Savior, my Lord. It is Your blood that changed everything. This book is for Your glory.

PART I – UNDERSTANDING THE RED LIGHT

~ 1 ~

STOPPED IN SHAME

The woman caught in adultery did not walk into that moment with confidence. She was dragged. Humiliated. Exposed. The people surrounding her weren't interested in her healing—they wanted her destruction. Their stones weren't just rocks in their hands; they were the weight of shame pressed upon her heart.

Shame works the same way in our lives. It paralyzes. It convinces us that we cannot go forward. It takes one moment of failure and tries to define an entire lifetime. It whispers: "You're not worthy. You're not good enough. You'll never recover."

Have you ever felt stopped in shame? Maybe it wasn't adultery. Maybe it was a broken promise, a failed marriage, a relapse, or a hidden habit. Whatever it was, you know the feeling of standing exposed before the world and wondering if life as you knew it is over.

But here is the truth: shame is not the same as conviction. Conviction comes from God to draw us closer to Him. Shame comes from the enemy to push us away from our destiny. Conviction says, "You did wrong, but you can be forgiven." Shame says, "You are wrong, and you will always be this way."

The difference is crucial. If we mistake shame for conviction, we will stop where we should keep going.

The Pause at the Red Light

Imagine driving through your city and coming to a red light. You stop, as you should. But then, even when it turns green, you never move. You sit there, motionless, while traffic piles up behind you. That is what shame does. It convinces us that the light has never changed.

The woman caught in adultery stood at such a light. Her accusers screamed "Stop! You have no future!" Yet Jesus stepped in to show her that the red of His blood was about to change everything.

Shame says stop. Grace says go.

Breaking the Chains of Shame

Shame often disguises itself as humility. It sounds like, "I'm just being honest about who I am." But true humility is not agreeing with the enemy's labels; it is agreeing with God's truth.

When you say, "I'm worthless," that is not humility—it's an insult to the God who created you. When you say, "I'll never change," that is not honesty—it's a denial of the cross that already made change possible.

Jesus broke the power of shame at Calvary. Hebrews 12:2 reminds us that He endured the cross, "despising the shame." That means shame tried to keep Him from His purpose, but He looked it in the eye and said, "You will not stop Me."

If Jesus despised the shame for you, you don't have to embrace it.

A Coaching Moment

In life coaching, we often talk about limiting beliefs—the lies we tell ourselves that keep us from progress. Shame is the root of many limiting beliefs. It convinces you that your failure is final. But here's the coaching truth: failure is an event, not an identity.

When coaching clients, I often ask: "If failure was your teacher instead of your prison guard, what would it be teaching you?" That question changes everything. Suddenly, the event that once brought shame becomes the lesson that produces growth.

You are not your mistake. You are not your worst moment. You are who God says you are—redeemed, restored, and released to go forward.

Moving from Stuck to Starting Again

The first step in breaking free from shame is acknowledging it. Name it. Bring it into the light. The woman in John 8 could not deny what she had done; the evidence was clear. But Jesus showed her that what was true did not have to remain her truth.

The second step is exchanging your labels for God's labels. Where you say, "I am guilty," God says, "You are forgiven." Where you say, "I am dirty," God says, "You are clean." Where you say, "I am broken," God says, "You are whole."

The third step is choosing to go. Shame will always give you reasons to stop: "What if you fail again? What if people talk? What if you're not ready?" But Jesus says, "Go. Sin no more."

Going doesn't mean you'll be perfect tomorrow. It means you'll no longer allow shame to park you at a red light that Jesus already turned green.

Momentum Moments (Life Coaching Exercises)

1. Name the Shame – Write down the areas of your life where you feel stopped in shame. Be honest. What moments from your past still whisper, "You can't move forward"?

_____

_____

_____

_____

2. Truth Exchange – Next to each statement of shame, write a Scripture truth that contradicts it. Example: Shame says: "I'm not forgiven." Truth says: "If we confess our sins, He is faithful and just to forgive us and cleanse us" (1 John 1:9).

- Shame says: _____
  Truth says: _____
- Shame says: _____
  Truth says: _____
- Shame says: _____
  Truth says: _____

3. Green Light Action – Identify one step you can take this week that represents moving forward. It could be a conversation, a journal entry, joining a group, or starting a new habit.

_____

_____

_____

_____

Declarations

Speak these aloud each day this week:

- I am not defined by my past; I am defined by God's promise.
- Shame is not my master; Jesus set me free.
- The red blood of Jesus gives me the green light to move forward.

• I am forgiven, loved, and empowered to go.

Prayer

Lord Jesus, thank You for despising the shame and carrying my sins to the cross. I lay down every label, every failure, and every regret at Your feet. I receive Your grace. I declare that I am free to go forward into my destiny. When shame whispers lies, let Your Spirit remind me of Your truth. Today, I choose to move. Amen.

~ 2 ~

THE CROWD AND THE STONES

When the woman caught in adultery was thrust before Jesus, she wasn't alone. A crowd had gathered. They weren't there to help her heal. They weren't there to offer her a second chance. They were there with stones in their hands—ready to make her failure final.

Every one of us has faced "the crowd." Sometimes that crowd is external—people who criticize, gossip, or hold your past over your head. Other times, the crowd is internal—the voices in your own mind that replay mistakes like a broken record. Either way, the stones feel real.

The crowd represents condemnation. The stones represent the harsh judgments of others. And both have the power to keep us stopped—if we allow them.

Condemnation from the Outside

Think about how quickly people judge. A single mistake can become the headline of your life. You may have done 99 things right, but people remember the 1 thing you got wrong. That's the nature of human judgment—it magnifies failure while minimizing progress.

The crowd around the woman had already decided her destiny: "Stone her. She deserves it." They weren't interested in her potential; they were obsessed with her punishment.

But Jesus didn't see what they saw. Where they saw a sinner to be condemned, He saw a daughter to be redeemed.

Condemnation from the Inside

Sometimes the loudest crowd is not outside but inside. Internal condemnation sounds like:

"I'll never change."

"I've messed up too much."

"God is done with me."

Those inner voices can be more destructive than the opinions of others because they come from within your own heart. Proverbs 23:7 reminds us, "As a man thinks in his heart, so is he." If you think like the crowd, you'll live like the condemned.

But Romans 8:1 declares: "There is therefore now no condemnation to those who are in Christ Jesus." Notice the word now. That means not tomorrow, not once you've proven yourself, not when you're perfect—right now.

The Coaching Perspective: Whose Voice Has the Mic?

As a life coach, I've seen people give the microphone of their life to the wrong voices. Imagine a stage where multiple people are lined up with microphones, but one voice is turned up louder than all the others. That's the one that controls the room.

The question is: whose voice has the mic in your life? Is it the crowd of critics? The stones of past mistakes? The inner dialogue of shame? Or is it the voice of Jesus—the only one who has the authority to define you?

Jesus silenced the crowd in John 8 by saying, "He who is without sin among you, let him throw a stone at her first." One by one, the stones dropped. Why? Because none of them were qualified to condemn.

Here's the coaching truth: the only One who could throw a stone at you chose instead to stretch His arms on a cross for you.

Releasing the Stones You Hold

It's easy to focus on the stones others hold against us, but sometimes we are the ones holding stones—against ourselves or even against others. When we refuse to forgive ourselves, we throw stones inward. When we hold grudges against others, we throw stones outward. Both keep us bound.

Jesus calls us to drop the stones. If He has forgiven us, who are we to keep throwing accusations?

Momentum Moments (Life Coaching Exercises)

1. Identify Your Crowd – Write down the external voices (people, groups, environments) that feed condemnation in your life. How do they speak? What do they say?

_____

_____

_____

_____

2. Recognize Your Stones – Reflect on the inner voices of condemnation. What do you say to yourself that keeps you stuck?

_____

_____

_____

_____

3. Shift the Mic – Choose one Scripture that represents God's voice and write it on a card or in your phone. Every time condemnation speaks this week, declare God's Word louder.

_____

_____

_____

_____

4. Forgiveness Practice – Drop a stone. Identify one area where you need to forgive yourself or another person. As a symbolic act, find a small stone, hold it in your hand, pray, and then drop it on the ground as a reminder that you're letting it go.

_____

_____

_____

_____

Declarations

Speak these aloud daily:

- I will not give the mic to the crowd of condemnation.
- The only One with the right to condemn me has chosen to forgive me.
- I drop the stones I've been holding against myself and others.
- There is no condemnation in Christ—I walk in freedom today.

Prayer

Father, thank You that no one has the power to condemn me because Jesus has already paid the price for my sins. Silence the voices of the crowd in my life, and amplify the voice of Your Spirit. Help me to drop the stones of self-hatred, guilt, and bitterness. Teach me to walk in the freedom that comes from Your forgiveness. I receive Your love, and I choose to go forward without fear. In Jesus' name, amen.

~ 3 ~

JESUS STEPS IN

The woman stood surrounded. A crowd ready to condemn her. Stones poised for release. Shame pressing like a weight too heavy to bear. In that moment, it looked like her story was finished.

But then—Jesus stepped in.

He bent down, writing in the dust, as the accusers demanded an answer. When He finally stood and spoke, everything shifted. One sentence from His mouth silenced the voices of condemnation:

"He who is without sin among you, let him throw a stone at her first" (John 8:7).

One by one, the stones dropped. One by one, the crowd dispersed. When Jesus stepped in, everything changed.

The Power of His Presence

What made the difference for the woman was not her own defense. She had no words. It wasn't her reputation—it had already been shattered. It wasn't the mercy of the crowd—they came to destroy, not to restore.

The difference was Jesus. His presence redefined the moment.

This is what He does for us. We cannot defend ourselves against every accusation. We cannot undo every mistake. But when Jesus steps in, He becomes our Advocate, our Defender, and our covering.

Hebrews 7:25 says, "He always lives to make intercession for them." That means right now, in this very moment, Jesus is stepping in for you before the Father.

The Coaching Perspective: Who Shows Up for You?

In coaching sessions, I often ask clients, "Who is in your corner when life gets tough?" Some respond with family, friends, or mentors. Others sadly admit they feel alone.

But here's the truth: the most important person who shows up for you is Jesus Himself. When everyone else walks out, He steps in.

The enemy wants you to believe you're abandoned in your failure. But the presence of Jesus proves otherwise. He shows up in the middle of the courtroom of life—not as your accuser but as your advocate.

Jesus Changes the Atmosphere

Notice what happened when Jesus entered the scene:
The focus shifted from the woman's sin to the crowd's hypocrisy.
The atmosphere shifted from judgment to reflection.
The outcome shifted from death to life.

When Jesus steps in, the atmosphere changes. That's why worship, prayer, and the Word are vital. They are not religious routines—they are environments that welcome His presence to shift the atmosphere of your life.

The Coaching Shift: From Victim to Victor

The woman could have remained a victim—forever labeled by her mistake. But because Jesus stepped in, her story shifted. She was no longer the adulterous woman defined by sin; she became the forgiven woman empowered to go.

Here's your coaching takeaway: When Jesus steps in, you shift from victim to victor.

Victims replay their pain. Victors rewrite their story.
Victims stay trapped in the past. Victors move toward their future.
Victims let others hold the pen. Victors let Jesus author their destiny.

Momentum Moments (Life Coaching Exercises)

1. Invite Him In – Reflect on one area of your life where you feel surrounded or accused. Write a prayer inviting Jesus to step in and take over.

_____

_____

_____

_____

2. Atmosphere Audit – What environments in your life invite Jesus' presence? Which ones push Him away? Make a plan to increase the first and decrease the second.

_____

_____

_____

_____

3. Victim or Victor? – List one situation where you've been seeing yourself as a victim. Then write a new narrative statement of how you will walk in victory because Jesus is stepping in.

Declarations

Speak these aloud each day this week:

- When Jesus steps in, the atmosphere changes in my life.
- I am not alone; my Advocate is with me.
- I shift from victim to victor because of His presence.
- The same Jesus who silenced the crowd silences every accusation against me.

Prayer

Lord Jesus, thank You for stepping into the broken places of my life. Where shame tried to silence me, You spoke words of freedom. Where others accused me, You defended me.

Where death waited for me, You gave me life. I invite Your presence into every corner of my heart and every situation I face. Step in, change the atmosphere, and lead me forward in victory. Amen.

Transition: From Red Light to Redemptive Power

We've walked with the woman caught in adultery. We've stood with her in shame, felt the sting of the crowd's stones, and breathed the relief of Jesus stepping in. Part I has shown us the reality of being stopped in life, surrounded by accusation, and then saved by the presence of Christ.

But the story doesn't end there. Jesus didn't just stop the crowd from stoning her—He empowered her with His words: "Go and sin no more."

That command was not possible in human strength. Left on her own, the woman would have fallen again. Left on our own, we would too. But here's the good news: Jesus never commands what He doesn't also empower.

The power to "go and sin no more" comes from His blood.

His blood is the reason condemnation has no hold on you.

His blood is the reason you can walk in freedom.

His blood is the reason your past is not your prison.

His blood is the reason red lights of shame turn into green lights of destiny.

In Part II, we will dive into the power of the blood. We will discover that every drop shed on Calvary speaks louder than shame, louder than failure, and louder than the voices of the crowd. His blood has a message: mercy, freedom, grace, and righteousness.

When the world says "red means stop," Heaven says through the blood of Jesus: "Red Means Go."

PART II – THE POWER OF THE BLOOD

~ 4 ~

RED MEANS MERCY

When the woman stood before Jesus, she deserved judgment. The law was clear. The evidence was undeniable. The crowd was ready to enforce the penalty. Yet, instead of stones, she received mercy.

Mercy is what happens when God does not give us what we deserve. Justice said she should die. Mercy said she could live. That is the power of the blood of Jesus. His blood cries out, not for condemnation, but for mercy.

Hebrews 12:24 tells us that Jesus' blood "speaks a better word than the blood of Abel." Abel's blood cried out for vengeance. Jesus' blood cries out for mercy. Every drop spilled at Calvary carries a message: "You are forgiven. You are covered. You are free."

Mercy Defined: The Stop That Saves

Mercy is God putting a stop to the punishment we rightfully deserve. Imagine standing in traffic, and a car speeds toward you. At the last second, a hand pulls you out of the way. That's mercy—it stops what was headed your way.

Mercy doesn't ignore sin. It acknowledges it but refuses to let sin have the final word. That's why Lamentations 3:22–23 says, "Through the Lord's mercies we are not consumed, because His compassions fail not. They are new every morning; great is Your faithfulness."

Every morning, the blood of Jesus declares: "You get to live again. You get another chance."

The Coaching Perspective: When Failure Meets Mercy

As a life coach, I often meet people stuck in cycles of regret. They replay their failures and rehearse their losses until they are paralyzed. But here's the truth: mercy interrupts the cycle.

Mercy means yesterday does not define today. Mercy means your last chapter is not your last chance. Mercy means there is still time to rebuild, restore, and recover.

When clients learn to receive mercy, their language shifts:

From "I can't believe I failed" to "I thank God I get to try again." From "I don't deserve another chance" to "God's mercies are new this morning."

From "I'm disqualified" to "I'm covered by the blood."

Mercy doesn't excuse wrong choices, but it empowers new ones.

Red Lights Rewritten by Mercy

Think about how the world interprets red: it means stop. But in God's Kingdom, the red of the blood means "stop condemnation, stop punishment, stop destruction." Mercy says:

Stop carrying shame.

Stop rehearsing regrets.

Stop punishing yourself.

Stop believing it's over.

When Jesus shed His blood, He rewrote the meaning of red. Now, red means go—go forward, go free, go into destiny.

Mercy and Identity

Here's something critical: mercy doesn't just forgive your act; it restores your identity.

The woman in John 8 was not remembered by Jesus as "the adulterous woman." To Him, she was a daughter worth saving. Mercy restores dignity. Mercy rewrites labels. Mercy shifts the conversation from what you did to who you are.

When you embrace mercy, you no longer walk around defined by your failures. You walk defined by His faithfulness.

Momentum Moments (Life Coaching Exercises)

1. Mercy Map – Take a sheet of paper and write down moments in your past where you know you deserved judgment, but God showed mercy. Reflect on how each moment became a stepping stone instead of a stumbling block.

_____

_____

_____

_____

2. Rewriting Red – On one side of a card, write the word RED. On the other, write "Mercy means go." Keep it in your wallet or purse as a daily reminder.

_____

_____

_____

_____

3. Mercy in Motion – This week, look for one person in your life who needs mercy. Offer forgiveness, patience, or grace instead of judgment. What you give will reinforce what you've received.

_____

_____

_____

_____

Declarations

Speak these aloud each day this week:

- The blood of Jesus covers me with mercy every day.
- I am not consumed because His compassions never fail.
- Red no longer means stop in my life—red means go.
- I walk in mercy, I receive mercy, and I extend mercy.

Prayer

Father, thank You for the mercy poured out through the blood of Jesus. Where I deserved judgment, You gave me forgiveness. Where I should have been stopped by my sin, You released me into freedom. Help me to live daily in the awareness of Your mercy. Teach me to show mercy to others as freely as You have shown it to me. Today, I declare that red means go, because Your mercy has rewritten my story. In Jesus' name, amen.

~ 5 ~

RED MEANS FREEDOM

One of the most powerful truths of the gospel is this: the blood of Jesus doesn't just forgive you, it frees you.

Forgiveness removes the penalty of sin. Freedom removes the power of sin.

The woman caught in adultery didn't just need pardon; she needed power. She needed the ability to walk out of that place without falling back into the same cycle. And that's exactly what Jesus gave her when He said, "Go and sin no more."

Galatians 5:1 declares: "It is for freedom that Christ has set us free. Stand firm, then, and do not let yourselves be burdened again by a yoke of slavery."

Through His blood, Jesus broke every chain that held you. The prison doors are open. The shackles are gone. The only question left is this: will you walk out free?

Freedom Defined: No Longer Bound

Freedom is more than the absence of chains; it's the presence of choice. Before Christ, sin ruled as a master. After Christ, you are empowered to choose righteousness.

Romans 6:14 says, "For sin shall not have dominion over you, for you are not under law but under grace." That means sin doesn't get the final say. Addiction doesn't get the final say. Generational curses don't get the final say. Grace does.

The blood of Jesus didn't just wipe your slate clean—it gave you authority to live differently.

The Coaching Perspective: Escaping Invisible Prisons

In coaching, I've worked with people who, though no physical chains hold them, live as if they're imprisoned. Their prison is invisible but powerful:

Fear keeps them locked up.

Guilt keeps them pacing in circles.

Lies keep them believing there's no escape.

But here's the coaching truth: freedom is not a feeling; it's a fact. You may not feel free, but if the Son has set you free, you are free indeed (John 8:36).

Your job is to align your mindset with the fact of your freedom. Coaching is about shifting perspective: from "I can't" to "I can through Christ." From "I'm stuck" to "I'm sent." From "I'm bound" to "I'm free."

Freedom vs. Familiarity

Sometimes, freedom feels uncomfortable because we've grown familiar with bondage. Like the Israelites longing for Egypt, it's tempting to go back to what we know rather than step into what is new.

But freedom requires courage. It demands new habits, new thinking, and new environments. If you want to live free, you must embrace the discomfort of change.

The woman could have gone back to the same places, the same patterns, the same people. But Jesus told her to go differently. Freedom meant new direction.

Living in Red's Freedom

The red blood of Jesus speaks a new language:
To fear, it says: "Stop!"
To shame, it says: "Stop!"
To bondage, it says: "Stop!"
But to you, it says: "Go free!"
Red no longer signals danger for your soul; it signals deliverance. Every time you remember the cross, you are reminded: freedom has been purchased.

Momentum Moments (Life Coaching Exercises)

1. Freedom Inventory – List areas in your life where you still feel bound (habits, mindsets, relationships). Ask: "Is this a prison Jesus already opened the door to?"

_____

_____

_____

_____

2. Rewrite the Script – For each area, write a freedom declaration rooted in Scripture. Example: "Fear has no hold on me, because God has not given me a spirit of fear" (2 Timothy 1:7).

3. Freedom Walk – Take a 15-minute walk this week with no distractions. As you walk, declare out loud: "I am free in Christ." Visualize leaving old chains behind with each step.

Declarations

Speak these aloud each day this week:

- Whom the Son sets free is free indeed.
- I am not a prisoner to sin, fear, or shame.
- The blood of Jesus has broken every chain in my life.
- I walk in freedom, and I will not go back to bondage.

Prayer

Father, thank You for the freedom purchased through the blood of Jesus. I declare that no chain, no addiction, and no fear has the power to hold me any longer. Teach me to walk boldly in the liberty You have given me. When the enemy tries to drag me back into bondage, remind me that the prison doors are already open. Today, I step into the freedom of Christ with confidence and joy. In Jesus' name, amen.

~ 6 ~

RED MEANS GRACE

Grace is one of the most beautiful gifts of God. Mercy holds back what we deserve; grace gives us what we don't deserve. Mercy stops the punishment; grace starts the blessing.

The woman caught in adultery experienced mercy when she wasn't stoned. But she also experienced grace when Jesus gave her a future. Mercy spared her life. Grace redirected her life.

Ephesians 2:8–9 reminds us: "For by grace you have been saved through faith, and that not of yourselves; it is the gift of God, not of works, lest anyone should boast." Grace cannot be earned; it must be received. It is God's undeserved favor poured out through the red blood of Jesus.

Grace Defined: The Power to Rise Again

Grace is not just pardon—it's power. It is not just forgiveness—it is fuel. Paul wrote in 1 Corinthians 15:10: "But by the grace of God I am what I am, and His grace toward me was not in vain; but I labored more abundantly... yet not I, but the grace of God which was with me."

Grace doesn't leave you where you are. Grace lifts you higher than you could ever climb on your own.

The Coaching Perspective: Permission to Grow

In life coaching, I've seen people get stuck because they don't give themselves permission to grow. They fear failure, so they don't try. They fear criticism, so they stay small. But grace is God's permission slip for growth.

Grace whispers:

"You don't have to be perfect—you just have to begin."

"You don't need to have it all together—God is holding you together."

"Your mistakes don't disqualify you—grace qualifies you."

Grace is not a license to sin. It is the power to overcome sin. It's the empowerment to live above your past and move toward your destiny.

The Woman's New Future

When Jesus said, "Go and sin no more," He wasn't just offering forgiveness; He was offering transformation.

That was grace.

The crowd said, "She is done." Jesus said, "She is destined." Grace rewrote her future in that moment.

Grace and Identity

Grace also redefines who you are. Without grace, you are simply a product of your past. With grace, you are a reflection of God's goodness.

Without grace: "I am a sinner trying to do better."

With grace: "I am the righteousness of God in Christ" (2 Corinthians 5:21).

Grace doesn't deny your past—it declares your future.

Momentum Moments (Life Coaching Exercises)

1. Grace Journal – Write down three areas where you feel unworthy. Next to each, write: "Grace covers this."

_____

_____

_____

_____

2. Grace Goals – Set one goal this week that you've been afraid to attempt because of fear of failure. Remind yourself: grace empowers me to try again.

_____

_____

_____

_____

3. Grace Statement – Create a personal declaration that starts with: "By the grace of God, I am..." Repeat it daily.

_____

_____

_____

_____

Declarations

Speak these aloud each day this week:

- I am who I am by the grace of God.
- Grace is greater than my mistakes.
- Grace empowers me to grow, rise, and move forward.

- The red blood of Jesus has given me the green light to live boldly.

Prayer

Father, thank You for Your amazing grace. Thank You that I don't have to earn it, perform for it, or qualify for it. Through the blood of Jesus, grace has found me, lifted me, and empowered me. Help me not to waste this gift but to live fully in it. When I feel unworthy, remind me that grace makes me worthy. Today, I step forward—not in my own strength but in the power of Your grace. In Jesus' name, amen.

~ 7 ~

RED MEANS RIGHTEOUSNESS

When the woman caught in adultery left the presence of Jesus, she walked away not only forgiven and free but also redefined. She was no longer identified by her mistake—she was covered by His righteousness.

This is the miracle of the blood of Jesus: it doesn't just wipe your record clean; it clothes you in His perfection.

Righteousness means being in right standing with God. Not because of your works, but because of His work on the cross.

2 Corinthians 5:21 says, "For He made Him who knew no sin to be sin for us, that we might become the righteousness of God in Him."

Through the blood of Jesus, there was an exchange: He took our sin, and we received His righteousness.

Righteousness Defined: Right Standing, Right Living

Righteousness has two sides:

Right Standing – the legal position we receive through Christ. This means God looks at you and sees Jesus' perfect obedience instead of your failures.

Right Living – the daily practice of walking out that righteousness. This means living in alignment with who God says you are.

You are not righteous because of what you do. You do right things because of who you are in Christ.

The Coaching Perspective: Identity Determines Action

In life coaching, identity is foundational. People live out of who they believe they are. If you believe you are broken, you will act broken. If you believe you are victorious, you will live victoriously.

That's why righteousness is so powerful. When you receive it, your identity shifts. You no longer see yourself as a sinner struggling to be holy—you see yourself as a saint empowered by grace.

The coaching truth is this: your actions will always rise to the level of your identity. When you embrace your righteousness in Christ, your behavior begins to align with your belief.

Covered by the Blood

Imagine standing before a judge guilty of every charge. Suddenly, someone steps in, pays your fine, and hands you a spotless record. That's justification. But righteousness goes even further—it clothes you in a new identity.

Isaiah 61:10 says, "He has clothed me with the garments of salvation, He has covered me with the robe of righteousness."

The red blood of Jesus is what produced this robe. When God looks at you, He doesn't see your failure—He sees His Son's perfection wrapped around you.

Living in Righteousness

To live in righteousness means:

- Walking in confidence, not condemnation.

- Making decisions that reflect who you are, not who you used to be.
- Refusing to let past failures dictate present choices.

The woman could leave her accusers not because she was suddenly flawless, but because she was covered. The same is true for you.

Momentum Moments (Life Coaching Exercises)

1. Identity Shift – Write down five statements you've believed about yourself that don't align with righteousness. Replace each with Scripture that declares your identity in Christ.

1. _____
2. _____
3. _____
4. _____
5. _____

2. Robe Reminder – Find a piece of clothing (a jacket, scarf, or robe). Each morning as you put it on, declare: "I am clothed in righteousness today."

3. Righteous Living Check-In – At the end of each day this week, reflect: Did my choices align with my righteous identity? What small shift can I make tomorrow?

Declarations

Speak these aloud each day this week:

- I am the righteousness of God in Christ Jesus.

- I am covered, forgiven, and made new through the blood.
- My actions flow from my righteous identity in Christ.
- The red blood of Jesus means I walk boldly in right standing with God.

Prayer

Father, thank You for the gift of righteousness purchased through the blood of Jesus. I could never earn it, but You freely gave it. Help me to live daily in the confidence of being clothed in righteousness. When the enemy tries to remind me of my past, let me remind him of the cross. Thank You that when You look at me, You see the righteousness of Your Son. Today, I choose to walk in that truth. In Jesus' name, amen.

Transition: From Covered to Commissioned

By now, we've looked closely at what the blood of Jesus accomplished for us. We've seen that red means mercy, red means freedom, red means grace, and red means righteousness. Each of these truths is life-changing on its own. Together, they create an unshakable foundation for your walk with God.

But here's the reality: the blood wasn't shed just so you could sit forgiven—it was shed so you could stand empowered. Jesus didn't cover you with mercy, grace, and righteousness so you could stay at the place of pardon. He covered you so you could go into the place of purpose.

When Jesus told the woman, "Go and sin no more," He wasn't just protecting her from the stones of the crowd. He was commissioning her into a new way of living. Her future didn't belong to shame—it belonged to grace-fueled destiny.

That's where Part III begins. Now that you understand the power of the blood, it's time to step into the command of Christ: **Go.**

Go in confidence.

Go in purpose.

Go in power.

Go in influence.

You're not leaving Part II with just head knowledge—you're carrying forward a lifestyle. The blood gives you permission to move, and the Spirit gives you power to keep moving.

So, let's step boldly into Part III. The next chapter will remind you that when Jesus says "Go," He also gives you confidence to take that first step.

PART III – GO AND SIN NO MORE

~ 8 ~

GO IN CONFIDENCE

When Jesus told the woman caught in adultery, "Go and sin no more," those words were not spoken timidly. He didn't say, "Go... if you think you can." He didn't whisper, "Go... but you'll probably fail again." No, His words carried authority and empowerment.

Confidence is the ability to move forward because you know who is backing you. The woman could walk away from her accusers because Jesus had spoken over her. His word replaced her shame with assurance. His blood replaced her guilt with grace. His presence replaced her fear with confidence.

That same confidence is available to you.

Confidence Defined: Assurance of Identity

Confidence is not arrogance. Arrogance depends on self. Confidence depends on God.

Arrogance says, "I've got this because I'm strong."
Confidence says, "I've got this because He is strong in me."

True confidence flows from identity. When you know who you are in Christ, you no longer have to second-guess every step. You can go boldly because you are rooted in His love and righteousness.

Hebrews 10:19 declares: "Therefore, brethren, having boldness to enter the Holiest by the blood of Jesus." Notice the source of our confidence: the blood.

The Coaching Perspective: Walking Past Fear

As a life coach, I've seen how fear paralyzes people. Fear says, "Don't move. Don't risk. Don't dream." Confidence says, "Go anyway."

Confidence is not the absence of fear—it's the decision to move forward in spite of fear. Courage is fear in motion.

Here's the coaching truth: you don't need full clarity to take your first step; you need confidence in the One who called you.

When the woman left Jesus, she didn't know all the details of her new future. But she knew one thing—He had set her free. That was enough to go.

Common Confidence Killers

Comparison – Looking at others and deciding you're not enough.

Condemnation – Listening to the voice of shame instead of the voice of grace.

Control – Believing you must know everything before you move.

Each of these killers keeps you at the red light. But Jesus says the light has changed.

How the Blood Builds Confidence

- The blood gives you access (Hebrews 10:19). You can approach God boldly without fear.
- The blood gives you assurance (Romans 5:9). You are justified and secure in His love.

- The blood gives you authority (Revelation 12:11). You overcome the enemy by the blood and your testimony.

Confidence is not about your resume—it's about His redemption.

Momentum Moments (Life Coaching Exercises)

1. Confidence Inventory – List three areas where you currently lack confidence. Next to each, write a truth from Scripture that empowers you in that area.

1. _____

2. _____

3. _____

2. Step of Faith – Choose one small but significant action this week that requires you to move forward in faith. Do it, even if you feel fear.

_____
_____
_____
_____

3. Confidence Anchor – Write a personal affirmation beginning with: "Because of the blood of Jesus, I can..." Repeat it daily.

_____
_____
_____
_____

Declarations

Speak these aloud each day this week:

- I go in confidence, not because of me, but because of Christ in me.
- Fear does not control me; faith leads me.
- The blood of Jesus gives me boldness to move forward.
- I walk with assurance because I know whose I am.

Prayer

Lord Jesus, thank You for the confidence that comes through Your blood. I don't have to live in fear, doubt, or hesitation. You have given me access, assurance, and authority. Silence the voices of comparison and condemnation in my life. Fill me with boldness to move forward into my destiny. Today, I declare that I will go in confidence because You are with me. In Your name I pray, amen.

~ 9 ~

GO IN PURPOSE

When Jesus told the woman, "Go and sin no more," He wasn't simply telling her to avoid repeating the same mistake. He was releasing her into a new direction. Her life was no longer defined by failure—it was redirected by purpose.

Purpose is the reason you exist. It is the assignment God placed in you before you were even born. Jeremiah 29:11 declares, "For I know the plans I have for you, declares the Lord, plans to prosper you and not to harm you, plans to give you a hope and a future."

The blood of Jesus doesn't just erase your past; it awakens your purpose.

Purpose Defined: God's Design, Not Human Demand

Purpose is not about impressing others. It's about fulfilling God's design. Too many people live chasing applause but miss their assignment. True purpose is discovered when you align your gifts, passions, and calling with God's plan.

Ephesians 2:10 says, "For we are His workmanship, created in Christ Jesus for good works, which God prepared beforehand that we should walk in them."

That means your purpose was planned before your failure. Your destiny was written before your mistake. Nothing you've done can erase what God wrote over your life.

The Coaching Perspective: Living on Assignment

In coaching, I often ask: "What wakes you up in the morning? What problem were you created to solve? Who benefits when you show up fully alive?"

Purpose is not about perfection; it's about direction. You don't have to have every detail figured out. You just have to move one step closer each day toward the assignment God has placed on your life.

Here's the coaching truth: purpose gives your "go" a destination. Without purpose, you wander. With purpose, you walk in destiny.

Purpose Breakers vs. Purpose Builders

Purpose Breakers: Fear, distraction, comparison, procrastination, people-pleasing.
Purpose Builders: Focus, faith, obedience, resilience, community.

If you feel stuck, ask yourself: Am I feeding the breakers or the builders?

The Woman's New Assignment

Though Scripture doesn't record the woman's future, imagine her testimony. She went from an object of shame to a witness of grace. That's purpose—to turn your story into someone else's hope.

Your purpose may not be public, but it will always be powerful. Whether it's raising children, leading teams, writing books, serving in ministry, or simply being a faithful light in your workplace, your purpose matters.

Momentum Moments (Life Coaching Exercises)

1. Purpose Statement – Write a one-sentence statement beginning with: "God created me to..." Don't overthink it—write what flows from your spirit.

_____

_____

_____

_____

2. Assignment Audit – List your current responsibilities. Which align with your God-given purpose, and which distract you?

_____

_____

_____

_____

3. Purpose Partner – Share your purpose statement with a trusted friend or mentor. Ask them to hold you accountable to living it out.

Declarations

Speak these aloud each day this week:

- I was created on purpose and for a purpose.
- The blood of Jesus empowers me to live in my divine assignment.
- My failures do not erase my destiny.
- Each step I take moves me closer to God's plan for my life.

Prayer

Father, thank You that my life has meaning beyond my mistakes. Thank You that Your purpose for me was written before the foundation of the world. Show me the assignments You have placed in my hands. Give me clarity to see, courage to pursue, and resilience to keep going. I declare that my life will bring glory to You as I walk in purpose. In Jesus' name, amen.

~ 10 ~

GO IN POWER

When Jesus told the woman to "Go and sin no more," He wasn't asking her to live differently in her own strength. Left to ourselves, we fail again and again. But when Jesus releases a command, He also provides the power to fulfill it.

This is why Acts 1:8 is so critical: "But you shall receive power when the Holy Spirit has come upon you; and you shall be witnesses to Me..." The blood of Jesus provides forgiveness, but the Spirit of Jesus provides power.

Together, they equip you to walk boldly into destiny.

Power Defined: Divine Ability in Human Weakness

Power is not about personality. It's not about being loud, bold, or naturally confident. Power is divine ability working through human weakness.

2 Corinthians 12:9 says, "My grace is sufficient for you, for My strength is made perfect in weakness." That means your weakness is not a disqualifier—it's a setup for His power.

When you go in power, you stop relying on what you can do and start relying on what God can do through you.

The Coaching Perspective: Energy vs. Power

Many people confuse energy with power. Energy is natural—it comes from sleep, diet, exercise, or mood. Power is supernatural—it comes from the Spirit.

Energy runs out. Power sustains.

Energy fluctuates. Power is steady.

Energy depends on you. Power depends on Him.

Here's the coaching truth: Your "Go" will wear out if it runs on energy, but it will last if it runs on power.

Power for Transformation

The woman didn't just need power to escape the crowd—she needed power to live a new life. The same is true for you. Power is what breaks the chains of addiction, lifts the weight of depression, and gives you boldness to step into places you thought were beyond you.

Romans 8:11 says, "The Spirit of Him who raised Jesus from the dead dwells in you..." Think about that: resurrection power lives inside you. If death couldn't hold Jesus, nothing can hold you when His Spirit is working through you.

How to Walk in Power

1. Stay Connected – Prayer, worship, and the Word keep you plugged into the Source.
2. Stay Surrendered – Power flows through yielded vessels, not resistant ones.
3. Stay Active – Power increases as you use it. The more you walk in obedience, the stronger it becomes.
4. The blood sets you free. The Spirit empowers you to stay free.

Momentum Moments (Life Coaching Exercises)

1. Weakness List – Write down three areas where you feel weakest. Pray and declare: "This is where His power shows up strongest."

1. _____

2. _____

3. _____

2. Power Activation – Identify one area where you've been relying on your own energy. This week, surrender it to God and ask for His Spirit's power.

_____

_____

_____

_____

3. Resurrection Reminder – Each morning this week, speak Romans 8:11 out loud: "The same Spirit that raised Jesus from the dead lives in me."

Declarations

Speak these aloud each day this week:

- I do not go in my own strength; I go in God's power.
- The Holy Spirit lives in me and empowers me daily.
- Where I am weak, His power is made perfect.
- I carry resurrection power into every situation of my life.

Prayer

Father, thank You that I am not called to live in my own strength. Thank You for sending the Holy Spirit to fill me with power. Teach me to stay connected to You, surrendered to Your will, and active in obedience. Let resurrection power flow through me to transform my life and impact others. Today, I go in power, knowing that nothing is impossible with You. In Jesus' name, amen.

~ 11 ~

GO IN INFLUENCE

The woman caught in adultery was once known for her shame. But after her encounter with Jesus, she carried a new story. Can you imagine her telling others, "I was dragged into the temple ready to die, but then Jesus stepped in, and everything changed"?

That testimony had influence. People who once looked at her as a sinner now had to reckon with her story of redemption.

You, too, are called to move from survivor to storyteller. Your influence flows through your willingness to share what Jesus has done.

How to Grow Your Influence

- Live Authentically – People are drawn to honesty. Your realness is more impactful than perfection.
- Serve Generously – Influence grows when you put others first.
- Speak Boldly – Share your story without shame. Someone is waiting to hear it.
- Stay Consistent – Influence is built over time, not in a single moment.

Momentum Moments (Life Coaching Exercises)

1. Ripple Reflection – Think of three people whose lives have been influenced by your choices or words. Write down how their lives changed.

1. _____

2. _____

3. _____

2. Story Practice – Write out your testimony in 3–5 sentences. Practice sharing it in a way that highlights God's work in your life.

_____

_____

_____

_____

3. Influence Intentionality – Choose one act of intentional influence this week—encourage someone, mentor someone, or serve someone in need.

Declarations

Speak these aloud each day this week:

- My life is a light that influences others for Christ.
- I move from survivor to storyteller.
- The blood of Jesus gives me influence beyond myself.
- My words and actions create ripples of transformation.

Prayer

Father, thank You for the influence You've entrusted to me. Help me to see my life as a testimony of Your grace. Give me boldness to share my story and humility to serve others. Let my influence point people, not to me, but to Jesus. May the ripples of my choices and words extend farther than I can see, leaving a legacy of faith. In Jesus' name, amen.

~ 12 ~

GO TO THE NATIONS

When Jesus told the woman, "Go and sin no more," He wasn't just speaking about her private behavior—He was releasing her into a public witness. Her life, once marked by shame, became a testimony of redemption.

In the same way, when Jesus sets you free, it's not only for your benefit. It's so your story can influence families, communities, cities, and ultimately, nations. The power of the blood is too great to be contained in your private world; it is meant to overflow into the world around you.

Jesus made this clear in Matthew 28:19-20: "Go therefore and make disciples of all the nations, baptizing them in the name of the Father and of the Son and of the Holy Spirit, teaching them to observe all things that I have commanded you..."

Your "Go" has global impact.

The Nations Defined: Beyond Your Borders

The nations don't just mean faraway countries. They mean people beyond your current circle. It could be your neighborhood, your workplace, your online community, or yes, even across oceans.

Acts 1:8 shows us the order: "...you shall be witnesses to Me in Jerusalem, and in all Judea and Samaria, and to the end of the earth." Start local. Expand outward. Influence global.

The Coaching Perspective: Enlarging Your Vision

As a coach, I've seen how small thinking limits big impact. Many people live with their eyes on survival instead of vision. But purpose without vision remains small.

Here's the coaching truth: When Jesus saves you, He doesn't just change your story—He enlarges your vision.

He wants you to think beyond paying bills, beyond daily routines, beyond personal struggles. He wants you to see yourself as a world-changer.

You may never step foot on foreign soil, but your prayers, your giving, your words, your influence can reach nations.

Living With a Global Mindset

To "Go to the Nations" means:

Live Missionally – Every space you enter becomes an opportunity for ministry.

Speak Boldly – Share Christ whenever doors open. Your story carries power.

Invest Generously – Support missions, ministries, and movements that advance the Gospel.

Pray Globally – Lift nations, leaders, and people groups before God. Prayer travels where your feet cannot.

The Woman's Ripple Effect

Though Scripture doesn't trace her journey, we can imagine that her encounter with Jesus didn't stay hidden. Her neighbors saw the difference. Her community whispered about her change. Her life became a testimony that spread farther than she knew.

Your story, too, can ripple outward—what Jesus does in you can't help but impact the world around you.

Momentum Moments (Life Coaching Exercises)

1. Vision Expansion – Write down three ways your life could influence people beyond your immediate circle (teaching, writing, mentoring, serving, etc.).

1. _____

2. _____

3. _____

2. Prayer Map – Pick three nations or people groups to pray for consistently over the next month.

1. _____

2. _____

3. _____

3. Mission Action – Find one practical way to support the Great Commission this week—through giving, volunteering, sharing your testimony, or mentoring someone in faith.

Declarations

Speak these aloud each day this week:

- My testimony is bigger than me—it impacts nations.
- I am part of God's global mission through the blood of Jesus.
- My influence extends beyond borders and generations.
- I go, not just locally, but with a vision for the nations.

Prayer

Father, thank You for calling me beyond myself. Thank You that the freedom You've given me is meant to ripple into the world around me. Give me a heart for the nations, a vision bigger than my own life, and a boldness to share the Gospel wherever I go. Use my story, my voice, my resources, and my influence to bring others into Your Kingdom. I declare that my life will touch nations, not by my strength, but by the power of Your Spirit. In Jesus' name, amen.

Transition: From Going to Growing

So far, we've walked with the woman caught in adultery and discovered what it means to encounter Jesus at the red light of shame. We've seen how His blood speaks mercy, freedom, grace, and righteousness. And in Part III, we embraced His command to "Go and sin no more"—to move forward in confidence, purpose, power, and influence, even extending to the nations.

But here's the truth: going is only sustainable if you keep growing. Many believers start strong but stall because they don't have the tools to maintain momentum. They know the "why" but struggle with the "how."

That's why Part IV matters. This section is where life- coaching principles meet biblical truth in practical steps. It's about learning how to:

Reset your mindset.

Build a destiny development plan.

Surround yourself with the right support systems.

Live out your freedom daily.

Recover quickly when you stumble.

Jesus didn't just want the woman to leave her past behind; He wanted her to build a future filled with wisdom, discipline, and purpose. The same is true for you.

If Parts I–III were about your encounter with Jesus, Part IV is about your engagement with life. It's where you take the truths you've learned and put them into motion—daily, consistently, and intentionally.

So let's step into the practical. Let's move from revelation to application. Let's learn how to grow strong in the freedom Jesus has given.

Next up is Chapter 13: Resetting Your Mindset, because before you can change your habits, you must first renew your mind.

PART IV – LIFE COACHING APPLICATION

~ 13 ~

RESETTING YOUR MINDSET

When Jesus told the woman, "Go and sin no more," He wasn't just pointing her feet in a new direction—He was renewing her mind. True transformation always begins in the mind.

Romans 12:2 says, "Do not be conformed to this world, but be transformed by the renewing of your mind, that you may prove what is that good and acceptable and perfect will of God."

A renewed mind sees differently. Where the old mindset said, "I'm a failure," the renewed mind says, "I'm forgiven." Where the old mindset said, "I'll always be stuck," the renewed mind says, "I'm free to move forward."

Resetting your mindset is the key to sustaining your freedom and walking in purpose.

Mindset Defined: The Filter of Your Life

Your mindset is the lens through which you see the world, yourself, and God. Two people can face the same situation and respond differently—not because of circumstances but because of mindset.

A negative mindset magnifies problems.
A faith mindset magnifies God.
A shame mindset keeps replaying failure.
A grace mindset keeps rehearsing forgiveness.

Your mindset shapes your choices, and your choices shape your destiny.

The Coaching Perspective: From Limiting Beliefs to Liberating Beliefs

In life coaching, we often deal with limiting beliefs—statements people repeat that lock them in place. They sound like:

"I'm not smart enough."

"I always fail."

"People like me never succeed."

These are prisons of the mind.

But through Christ, we replace limiting beliefs with liberating beliefs—truths from God's Word that unlock forward motion:

"I have the mind of Christ" (1 Corinthians 2:16).

"I can do all things through Christ who strengthens me" (Philippians 4:13).

"Nothing can separate me from the love of God" (Romans 8:39).

Here's the coaching truth: the greatest battle you will ever fight is the one between your ears. Victory begins in your thought life.

Steps to Reset Your Mindset

1. Recognize the Lies – Pay attention to the thoughts that dominate your mind. Are they aligned with God's truth or the enemy's lies?

2. Replace with Truth – For every lie, find a Scripture that declares the opposite. Speak it until it becomes your default thought.

3. Renew Daily – Resetting your mindset is not a one-time event; it's a daily practice of aligning your thoughts with God's Word.

The Woman's Reset

Think about it: the woman could have left Jesus still carrying shame in her mind. She could have walked away forgiven but still believing she was unworthy. But His words, "Neither do I condemn you," reset her mindset.

That's the key—your outward freedom will never outpace your inward mindset. If you don't think new, you won't live new.

Momentum Moments (Life Coaching Exercises)

1. Thought Journal – For three days, track your recurring thoughts. At the end of each day, sort them into two columns: Truth or Lie.

Day 1

_____

_____

_____

_____

_____

_____

_____

_____

_____

_____

_____

_____

Day 2

_____

_____

Day 3

Truths	

2. Mindset Reset Card – Write your top three limiting beliefs on one side of a card. On the other side, write three liberating Scriptures. Keep the card with you and review it daily.

1. _____

2. _____

3. _____

3. Morning Mindset Ritual – Begin each morning with one declaration, one Scripture, and one prayer that align your mind with God's truth.

_____

_____

_____

_____

Declarations

Speak these aloud each day this week:

- I have the mind of Christ, and I think His thoughts about me.
- I reject limiting beliefs and embrace God's liberating truth.
- Every day my mind is being renewed by the Word of God.
- My mindset is shifting from shame to grace, from fear to faith.

Prayer

Father, thank You that transformation begins in my mind. Today, I surrender every limiting belief, every lie of the enemy, and every thought that keeps me stuck. Replace them with Your truth. Give me the discipline to renew my mind daily in Your Word. Let my mindset reflect who I am in Christ, not who I was in the past. I declare that my thoughts align with Your promises, and my life will follow. In Jesus' name, amen.

~ 14 ~

DESTINY DEVELOPMENT PLAN

Forgiveness is the doorway. Freedom is the atmosphere. Grace is the fuel. Righteousness is the identity. But purpose is the path — and paths require a plan.

When Jesus told the woman to "Go and sin no more," He didn't hand her a detailed life map. He gave her freedom and direction. But for her to walk into destiny, she needed more than good intentions — she needed intentional steps.

This is where the Destiny Development Plan comes in.

Proverbs 29:18 says, "Where there is no vision, the people perish." A vision without a plan remains a dream. But when vision is broken down into practical steps, it becomes destiny in motion.

Destiny Defined: God's Blueprint for Your Life

Destiny is not random. It's God's designed outcome for your life. He has already prepared the works you are to walk in (Ephesians 2:10). But walking them out requires discipline, focus, and structure.

Think of destiny like a seed. Inside a seed is the full picture of a tree, but without the right soil, water, and sunlight, the seed will never grow. A Destiny Development Plan is the environment that allows your calling to flourish.

The Coaching Perspective: From Wishful Thinking to Strategic Living

Many people live with vague statements like:

"One day I'll start a business."

"Someday I'll write that book."

"I know God wants to use me somehow."

But in coaching, vague hopes become specific goals.

"Someday" becomes a calendar date.

"Somehow" becomes an action step.

"Maybe" becomes measurable progress.

Here's the coaching truth: God gives vision, but you must build structure. Faith sets the direction, but planning sets the pace.

The Three Components of a Destiny Plan

1. **Clarity (What is God calling you to do?)**
   - Write it down. Be specific. Habakkuk 2:2 says, "Write the vision and make it plain."
   - Example: Instead of "I want to help people," write, "I will mentor young adults in faith and leadership."

2. **Commitment (What steps will you take?)**
   - Break your vision into actionable goals.
   - Example: If your destiny involves writing, commit to writing 500 words a day.

3. **Consistency (How will you stay on track?)**
   - Build habits and accountability. Destiny isn't reached in one giant leap; it's reached by faithful steps over time.

The Woman's Plan

Though Scripture doesn't record her next steps, we know she couldn't go back to the same environment, same choices, or same circle. Her plan needed to include:

- New people who spoke life instead of condemnation.
- New places that supported her future, not her past.
- New practices that aligned with her new identity.

That's what destiny planning looks like—intentionally shifting life to align with freedom.

Momentum Moments (Life Coaching Exercises)

1. Write the Vision – Take 10 minutes to write down one destiny goal you sense God calling you to. Be specific and clear.

_____

_____

_____

_____

2. Break It Down – Write three action steps you can take in the next 30 days toward that destiny.

1. _____

2. _____

3. _____

3. Accountability Partner – Share your vision and first steps with someone you trust. Ask them to check in with you weekly.

Declarations

Speak these aloud each day this week:

- God has a blueprint for my life, and I will walk in it.
- I move from vague dreams to specific action.
- My destiny is not someday—it begins today with faithful steps.
- I am focused, committed, and consistent in pursuing God's plan.

Prayer

Father, thank You for the destiny You designed for me before I was even born. I ask for clarity to see the vision, courage to commit to the steps, and consistency to keep moving forward. Align my habits, relationships, and environments with my calling. Let my Destiny Development Plan be more than paper—let it be a life lived in obedience to You. In Jesus' name, amen.

* * *

No one fulfills destiny alone. Even the woman caught in adultery couldn't walk out her new life in isolation. She had to surround herself with people who would support her freedom, not sabotage it.

God never designed us to grow in solitude. From Genesis onward, the pattern is clear: "It is not good for man to be alone" (Genesis 2:18). Isolation breeds weakness, but accountability builds strength.

Proverbs 27:17 says, "As iron sharpens iron, so one person sharpens another." Without the right people in your life, your purpose will dull. With the right people, your potential will sharpen.

~ 15 ~

ACCOUNTABILITY & SUPPORT SYSTEMS

Accountability is not control. It's not someone micromanaging your life. Accountability is mutual agreement for growth. It's saying, *"I want to go higher, and I'm giving you permission to call me upward."*

Accountability partners ask hard questions.
Mentors provide guidance from experience.
Community offers encouragement and belonging.

Together, they form a support system that keeps you moving when you'd rather quit.

The Coaching Perspective: The Power of the Circle

In coaching, we often say, *"Show me your circle, and I'll show you your future."* The five people you spend the most time with will shape your mindset, habits, and destiny.

Here's the coaching truth: **You cannot soar with eagles if you keep walking with chickens.**

Ask yourself:
Are the people around me pulling me forward or holding me back?
Are they sharpening my faith or dulling it?

Biblical Models of Support Systems

Moses had Aaron and Hur (Exodus 17:12). When his arms grew tired, they held them up.

David had Jonathan (1 Samuel 18:3-4). Jonathan strengthened him in the Lord.

Paul had Timothy (2 Timothy 1:2). He poured into him for generational impact.

Jesus had the disciples (Luke 6:13). He walked with twelve, but invested deeply in three.

Even Jesus didn't walk alone. Why should we?

Building Your Support System

1. **Identify Your Inner Circle** – Who are the voices you allow closest to your heart? Do they align with your destiny?
2. **Seek Wise Mentorship** – Find someone who has walked the path you're pursuing and learn from their wisdom.
3. **Establish Accountability Partners** – Choose people who love you enough to be honest, even when it stings.
4. **Commit to Community** – Join a church, small group, or network that reinforces your growth.

The Woman's Support

The woman Jesus forgave needed new connections. If she returned to the same environment that fueled her sin, she would stumble again. Her "go and sin no more" required new people who spoke life.

The same is true for you. Your support system can either reinforce your old patterns or propel you into your destiny. **Choose wisely.**

Momentum Moments (Life Coaching Exercises)

1. Circle Check – Write down your five closest relationships. Ask: *Do they sharpen me, drain me, or distract me?*

1. _____

2. _____

3. _____

4. _____

5. _____

2. Mentor Move – Identify one person who could serve as a mentor in your life. Reach out to them this week.

_____

_____

_____

_____

3. Accountability Ask – Choose one trustworthy friend and say, *"Will you hold me accountable to this goal?"*

Declarations

Speak these aloud each day this week:

- I am not called to walk alone—God has placed people in my life to sharpen me.
- My circle reflects my destiny, and I choose wisely who speaks into me.

- Accountability is not control—it is strength for my journey.
- I go further, faster, and stronger because of the right support system.

Prayer

Father, thank You that You never intended for me to walk alone. Place the right people around me—mentors, partners, and community—that will sharpen my faith and strengthen my purpose. Give me discernment to release relationships that hold me back and embrace those that propel me forward.

Help me to be accountable, teachable, and faithful. In Jesus' name, amen.

~ 16 ~

LIVING REDEMPTIVELY DAILY

It's one thing to experience forgiveness in a single moment. It's another to live out redemption every day. The woman caught in adultery had a life-changing encounter with Jesus, but she still had to wake up the next morning and live in her new reality.

That's where many of us struggle. We believe in redemption on Sunday, but by Monday, the weight of life tries to pull us back. The key to lasting transformation is learning to live redemptively every single day.

Living Redemptively Defined: Walking Out What He Already Finished

To live redemptively means to let the finished work of Jesus shape your daily choices. It's not about striving for approval; it's about living from acceptance.

Redemption says: "You are bought back."
Daily living says: "Now walk like you belong."

1 Corinthians 6:20 reminds us: "You were bought at a price. Therefore honor God with your bodies."

You are no longer your own. You belong to Him—and that reality should shape how you think, speak, and act.

The Coaching Perspective: From Big Leap to Daily Steps

In coaching, we emphasize that change doesn't stick unless it's broken down into daily steps. Grand declarations are powerful, but habits determine direction.

Here's the coaching truth: lasting transformation is the result of daily disciplines, not occasional inspiration.

Anyone can feel redeemed in a powerful church service. Living redeemed means building small, consistent habits that align with your new identity.

Daily Practices for Redemptive Living

1. **Start with Scripture** – Renew your mind with God's Word each morning. Let truth set the tone for your day.
2. **Pray Throughout the Day** – Prayer doesn't have to be long; it just has to be consistent. Stay connected to your Redeemer.
3. **Guard Your Inputs** – What you watch, listen to, and consume either feeds your redemption or fights it.
4. **Serve Someone** – Redemption isn't just about you; it's about letting your freedom bless others.
5. **Reflect at Night** – End your day by asking, "Did my life today reflect the One who redeemed me?"

The Woman's New Routine

We don't know the details of her life after that day, but one thing is certain: she couldn't live the same way she had before. She had to create new rhythms—places she no longer visited, people she no longer entertained, and practices that kept her grounded in freedom.

Your daily redemption looks the same. It's not about perfection—it's about progress. Each day you choose to live as the redeemed, you reinforce your new identity.

Momentum Moments (Life Coaching Exercises)

1. Redemptive Rhythm – Design a simple morning and evening routine that reminds you of your redemption. Example: Scripture + prayer in the morning, reflection + gratitude at night.

_____

_____

_____

_____

2. Input Audit – For one week, track what you watch, listen to, and read. Ask: "Does this feed or fight my redemptive identity?"

- Sunday:

_____

- Monday:

_____

- Tuesday:

_____

- Wednesday:

_____

- Thursday:

_____

- Friday:

_____

- Saturday:

_____

3. Serve Once Daily – Commit to one small act of service each day this week—an encouraging word, a helping hand, or a prayer for someone in need.

- Sunday:

  _____

- Monday:

  _____

- Tuesday:

  _____

- Wednesday:

  _____

- Thursday:

  _____

- Friday:

  _____

- Saturday:

  _____

Declarations

Speak these aloud each day this week:

- I live redemptively every day, not just in moments of inspiration.
- I am bought with a price, and I honor God with my life.
- My daily habits reflect my redeemed identity in Christ.
- Each day is an opportunity to walk in freedom and shine His light.

Prayer

Father, thank You that redemption is not a moment but a lifestyle. Teach me to walk daily in the reality of what Jesus has finished for me. Help me build rhythms, habits, and choices that reflect my identity as redeemed. When I'm tempted to drift back into old patterns, remind me that I am bought with a price and set apart for Your glory. Let every day of my life be an offering that honors You. In Jesus' name, amen.

~ 17 ~

WHEN YOU STUMBLE AGAIN

Let's be honest: freedom doesn't mean perfection. Even after a powerful encounter with Jesus, there will be days when you stumble. The enemy will whisper, "See? Nothing has really changed." Shame will try to creep back in. Old patterns may resurface.

But here's the truth: stumbling does not mean you are back in chains. Falling does not mean you have failed permanently. Proverbs 24:16 reminds us: "For though the righteous fall seven times, they rise again."

The key is not avoiding every stumble—the key is learning how to rise again.

The Reality of Stumbling

The woman Jesus forgave had a real choice after she left Him. She could embrace her new life, or she could slip back into old ways. Jesus knew this, which is why His words "Go and sin no more" carried both a challenge and a promise.

He wasn't just telling her to never make a mistake again; He was telling her that His grace would be present when she did.

The Coaching Perspective: Fail Forward

In coaching, we talk about failing forward. This means using every stumble as a stepping stone instead of a stumbling block.

Failure teaches lessons success never could.

Failure builds resilience.

Failure refines focus.

Here's the coaching truth: falling is not the opposite of progress—quitting is. As long as you rise again, you are still moving toward destiny.

How to Respond When You Stumble

1. **Recognize Quickly** – Don't hide. Admit your mistake before God.
2. **Repent Fully** – Turn back to Him with sincerity, not shame.
3. **Receive Grace** – Remember 1 John 1:9: "If we confess our sins, He is faithful and just to forgive us."
4. **Reset Your Mindset** – Replace lies of condemnation with truth from God's Word.
5. **Resume the Journey** – Take the next step forward. Don't stay down.

The Enemy's Trap vs. God's Truth

1. **Enemy's Trap:** "You failed again—you're worthless."
2. **God's Truth:** "You stumbled, but you're still righteous in Christ."
3. **Enemy's Trap:** "Give up—this isn't working."
4. **God's Truth:** "Rise again—My grace is sufficient."

Momentum Moments (Life Coaching Exercises)

1. Failure Journal – Write down one past stumble. List the lesson it taught you. Then declare how it has strengthened you moving forward.

_____

_____

_____

_____

2. Grace Reset – Each time you stumble this week, immediately pause and declare out loud: "I am forgiven. I rise again."

3. Bounce-Back Plan – Write out 3 steps you will take the next time you stumble (e.g., pray immediately, call an accountability partner, review your declarations).

1. _____

2. _____

3. _____

Declarations

Speak these aloud each day this week:

- I may stumble, but I will not stay down.
- Failure is not my identity; righteousness is my identity.
- The grace of God lifts me every time I fall.
- I rise again, stronger and wiser after every stumble.

Prayer

Father, thank You that stumbling does not separate me from Your love. Thank You that Your grace covers me when I fall. Teach me to rise quickly, repent sincerely, and walk forward boldly. Protect me from the enemy's lies of condemnation, and remind me that my destiny is greater than my mistakes. Today, I declare that I may stumble, but I will not quit. By Your grace, I rise again. In Jesus' name, amen.

Transition: From Application to Acceleration

You've walked through the red light of shame, discovered the power of the blood, and received Jesus' command to "Go and sin no more." You've learned how to reset your mindset, develop your destiny plan, build support systems, live redemptively each day, and even rise again when you stumble.

By now, you've seen that this journey isn't about staying stuck—it's about moving forward. Not in your strength, but in His. Not in fear, but in faith. Not in shame, but in freedom.

The red of His blood has rewritten the rules. What once meant stop now means go. You are no longer condemned. You are commissioned. You are no longer bound. You are becoming.

But the journey doesn't end here. Everything has been leading to this moment—the Final Green Light. It's where revelation turns into acceleration. It's where you step boldly into the fullness of your God-given destiny, leaving hesitation behind forever.

The next chapter is not just a conclusion; it's a commissioning. It's the Spirit of God whispering and shouting at once: "The light is green. Red means go. Step into the life I've called you to."

CLOSING CHAPTER

~ 18 ~

THE FINAL GREEN LIGHT

Traffic lights are designed to regulate movement. Red means stop. Yellow means slow down. Green means go.

But in the Kingdom of God, something radical happened at the cross. The blood of Jesus turned red into the ultimate "Go." The shame that once stopped you has been erased. The guilt that once slowed you has been removed. And now the Spirit of God is waving you forward with the Final Green Light.

When Jesus told the woman, "Neither do I condemn you; go and sin no more," He gave her permission to move into destiny. Today, He gives you the same command. You are free to go forward. Not cautiously, not halfway, not looking over your shoulder—but boldly, confidently, and joyfully into the life He has prepared for you.

What the Final Green Light Means

Permission to Move Forward

- No more waiting at the red light of shame.
- No more circling the same intersection of regret.
- The light has changed—you are cleared for progress.

Power to Live Differently

- You don't move in your own strength; you move in resurrection power.
- Every step is fueled by grace and guided by the Spirit.

Purpose Bigger Than You

- Your "Go" isn't just about escaping sin; it's about fulfilling destiny.
- Nations, communities, and families are waiting for your obedience.

The Coaching Perspective: Your Launch Moment

In coaching, there comes a point where enough preparation has been done. The plan is written, the mindset is reset, the accountability is in place—and now it's time to launch.

The Final Green Light is your launch moment. No more excuses. No more delays. No more living in "someday." Today is your green light.

Here's the coaching truth: **The worst place to live is at the intersection of "what was" and "what could be."**
The green light is God's signal to leave *what was* behind and enter *what will be.*

Biblical Confidence in the Green Light

"Forgetting those things which are behind and reaching forward to those things which are ahead" (Philippians 3:13).
"The steps of a righteous man are ordered by the Lord" (Psalm 37:23).
"Now to Him who is able to do exceedingly abundantly above all that we ask or think" (Ephesians 3:20).

Each of these verses is a green light from Heaven, urging you to move.

Momentum Moments (Life Coaching Exercises)

1. Green Light Commitment – Write down one area where you've been stalled. Declare: "The light is green—I move forward today." Then take one step within 24 hours.

_____

_____

_____

_____

2. Vision Prayer Walk – Take a walk while praying over your future. Speak out loud what you believe God has called you to. Visualize crossing through the intersection into destiny.

3. Legacy Letter – Write a letter to your future self, describing the life you will live because you obeyed the green light. Keep it as a reminder of what's possible.

_____

_____

_____

_____

_____

_____

_____

_____

_____

_____

_____

_____

_____

_____

_____

_____

_____

_____

_____

_____

_____

Declarations

Speak these aloud each day this week:

- The blood of Jesus has turned every red light of shame into a green light of destiny.
- I am released to go forward—confidently, powerfully, and purposefully.
- Nothing in my past can stop what God has placed in my future.
- Today, I accept the Final Green Light and step boldly into my destiny.

Prayer

Father, thank You for the cross where red became my green light. Thank You for mercy that spared me, grace that lifted me, righteousness that covered me, and power that filled me. I declare today that I will not remain stuck at the light of shame or hesitation. I receive Your Final Green Light to move into my destiny.

Guide my steps, strengthen my heart, and let my life shine as a testimony of Your redemption.

Today, I go—boldly, joyfully, and fully alive in Christ. In Jesus' name, amen.

A Final Word from the Author

My friend, the light is green. You've carried the lessons, the Scriptures, the declarations, and the strategies. Now it's time to step out of hesitation and into acceleration.

Don't wait for perfect conditions. Don't wait for unanimous approval. Don't wait for all the answers. Go.

The blood of Jesus has already changed the light. And remember always: Red Means Go.

Dr. Tony Medley Sr. is a pastor, teacher, mentor, and author whose life and ministry have been dedicated to helping people discover the power of God's Word spoken over their lives. Known for his passionate preaching and practical teaching, Dr. Medley has spent decades equipping believers to hear God's voice, walk in their identity in Christ, and live with purpose and bold faith. His ministry extends beyond the pulpit—through books, training materials, stage plays, and discipleship resources—designed to ignite transformation in individuals, churches, and communities.

Dr. Medley combines deep biblical insight with everyday application, ensuring that readers not only understand the Scriptures but also live them out with confidence. With a message that is both prophetic and practical, Dr. Medley inspires people to see themselves through heaven's perspective. He believes every person is "wrapped in the conversation" of God and destined to thrive in His promises.

When he is not writing or teaching, Dr. Medley is serving his church family, mentoring emerging leaders, and enjoying time with his own family, who remain his greatest earthly joy.

www.ingramcontent.com/pod-product-compliance
Lightning Source LLC
Chambersburg PA
CBHW051543120626
46551CB00013B/1347